HYGGE

Enjoy The Present Moment
With a High Vibe & Have No Stress

HYGGE

Hygge could be considered a fulfillment. It carries a modest stillness of the mind and a deep tribal force. In essence, hygge means creating a warm atmosphere and enjoying the good things in life with lovely people.

Like sitting on a cozy sofa reading your favourite book, while holding a cup of warm chai latte, legs curled up in a fluffy blanket. Candles flickering and the sweet scent of cinnamon buns filling the air. Now this is hygge.

The origins of Danish hygge

Hygge (pronounced hoo-gah) didn't originate in the Danish language but in old Norwegian, where it meant something like "well-being." It first appeared in Danish writing around the end of the 18th Century and the Danes have embraced it ever since.

Live in the Moment

"Do what you can, with what you have, where you are."
— Theodore Roosevelt

It could be something as small as having a cup of herbal tea and enjoying a few moments of silence. Taking a short walk and saying affirmations. Taking a nap, listening to relaxing music, reading a few chapters of your favorite book, pulling weeds and planting seeds in your garden, spending quality time with your pets, cutting fresh flowers and making floral arrangements to beautify your space. There are literally endless amounts of things you can do.

"With every breath,
I plant the seeds of devotion,
I am a farmer of the heart."
— Rumi

AUTUMN HYGGE

- Good books
- Hot drinks
- Oven baked bread
- Rainy days
- Aroma sauna
- Soothing bath
- Sensation of change
- Self-Reflection
- Warm candlelight
- Embroidery
- Scent of pine trees in the rain

Which is your autumn hygge?

Dipping your steaming toes in the crisp autumn lake...
Running barefeet across the wooden steps of a misty bog..
just before an unexpected dip.
Filling your lungs with the crisp fresh air after coming
from the rejuvenating smoky sauna.

The Nordic Sauna Rituals:

- Garlic scent.
- Frozen orange slices.
- Sauna yoga.
- Beating each other with thin birch tree branches!
- Naked freedom run.
- Icy sea-buckthorn juice.

Dancin' with the premiscuous winds of life among the fields of gold...

"I am so thirsty for the marvelous that only the marvelous has power over me."
— Anais Nin

"Do you think I know what I'm doing? That for one breath or half-breath I belong to myself? As much as a pen knows what it's writing, or the ball can guess where it's going next."
—Rumi

Surrender to the self!

"My ideas usually come not at my desk writing but in the midst of living."
— Anais Nin

"The role of a writer is not to say what we all can say, but what we are unable to say."
— Anais Nin

"If you do not breathe through writing, if you do not cry out in writing, or sing in writing, then don't write, because our culture has no use for it."
— Anais Nin

The Bookshelf That Makes You SMILE :)

- Take all your books out of the shelf.
- Find your favorite way of organising them.
- Alphabetical / By color /By Genre / By Rating.
- Make sure it feels just right so that every time you go home, you feel happy!

"Consider how wool is turned into an elegantly designed carpet by coming into contact with an intelligent person."
— Rumi

"I can't stop pointing to the beauty. Every moment and place says, 'Put this design in your carpet!!"
— Rumi

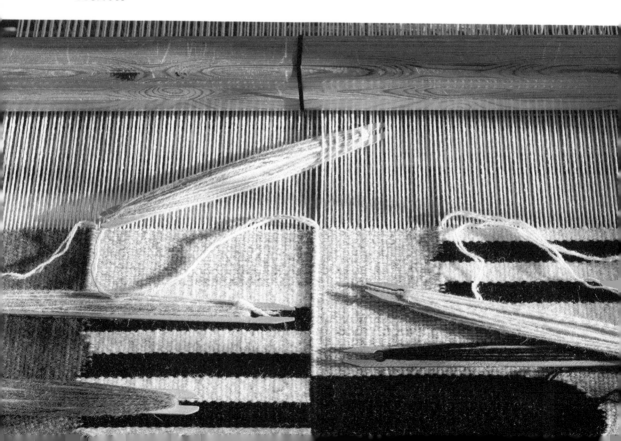

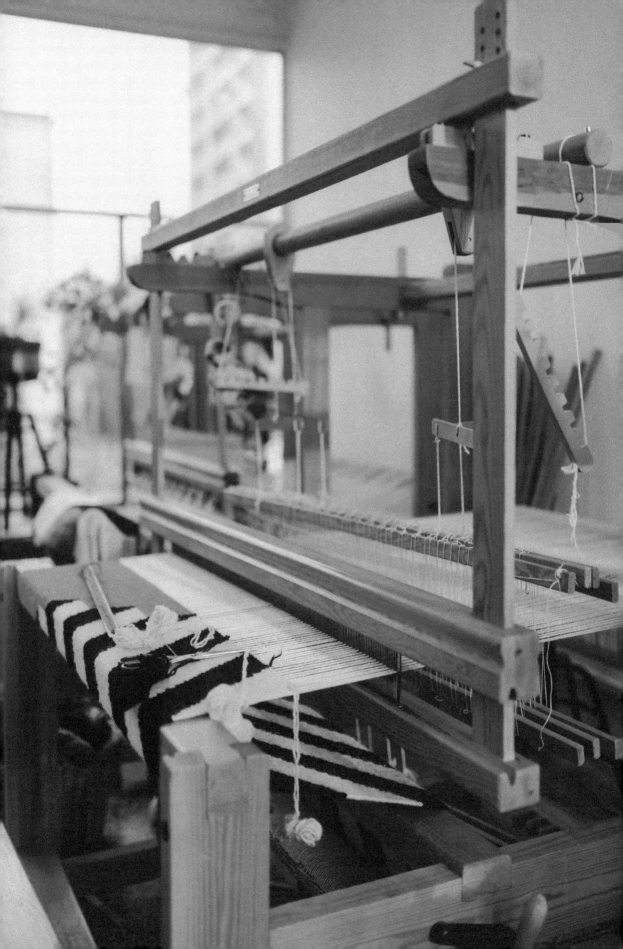

Forge your very own creativity-boosting zone at home.

Get creative and express yourself in whatever way you like. Painting, writing, sculpting, building, music, whatever takes your fancy, and make sure you leave your inner critic at the door. There are no right ways to be creative.

After a burst of creativity you can almost feel the glimmer of passion in the room. It's the feeling that truly makes you feel alive!

WILLIAM SHAKESPEARE SONNET 24

Mine eye hath played the painter and hath steeled
Thy beauty's form in table of my heart.
My body is the frame wherein 'tis held,
And pérspective it is best painter's art.
For through the painter must you see his skill
To find where your true image pictured lies,
Which in my bosom's shop is hanging still,
That hath his windows glazèd with thine eyes.
Now see what good turns eyes for eyes have done:
Mine eyes have drawn thy shape, and thine for me
Are windows to my breast, wherethrough the sun
Delights to peep, to gaze therein on thee.
Yet eyes this cunning want to grace their art;
They draw but what they see, know not the heart.

"This moment contains all moments."
— C.S.Lewis

"There are books which we read early in life, which sink into our consciousness and seem to disappear without leaving a trace. And then one day we find, in some summing-up of our life and put attitudes towards experience, that their influence has been enormous."
— Anais Nin

Music is food for the soul and an instant way to gain peace of mind.

- Listening to music
- Singing along to music
- Moving to the beat of the music
- Playing an instrument
- Meditating

It is the body's vibrations which ripple from the fingers.

BANANA BREAD

Want to make someone's day? Bake them some banana bread!

- 1 Stick (1/2 Cup) Butter
- 3 Large Ripe Bananas
- 2 Large Eggs
- 1 teaspoon Vanilla Extract
- 2 Cups All Purpose Flour
- 1 Cup Granulated Sugar
- 1 teaspoon Baking Soda
- 1/2 teaspoon salt
- 1/2 teaspoon cinnamon

- Heat the oven to 350°F and prep the pan.
- Melt the butter.
- Combine the butter and sugar.
- Add the eggs
- Add the milk and vanilla.
- Mash in the bananas.
- Add the flour, baking soda, and salt.
- Fold in the nuts or chocolate, if using.
- Pour the batter into the pan.
- Bake for 50 to 65 minutes.
- Cool in the pan for 10 minutes.
- Remove from pan and cool another 10 minutes.

Your pets are the equivalent to Your soul — they see you and know what You really need.

Make the effort of knowing what they truly need.

Sleep is what replenishes the spirit.
Healthy food keeps them energized.
Your pets deserve the gentle touch they have come to love, do not forget that.
Some pets, cats for example, also need their space, but you probably alrealdy knew that.

The fingers play out the melody of our personal story.

The tips are like a conductor's cane and the keyboard is though an orchestra.

"Falling leaves hide the path so quietly."
— John Bailey

The traditional art of Mushroom Hunting has been cultivated and inherited by a long line of generations.

Season of mists and mellow fruitfulness.

Nothing beats the subtle sunlight creeping in on a warm evening with the smell of apple pie revolving around your cozy home!

The feeling of your ancestors looking over you, blessing your life. Feelings of gratitude for having built such a wondersful life.

The only thing you need is a glass of fresh apple juice.

Apples carry the nectar of life.
Cool moss knows the essence
of your soul.
The blue sky has seen it all.
Look inside — so do YOU.

"A leaf fluttered in through the window this morning, as if supported by the rays of the sun, a bird settled on the fire escape, joy in the task of coffee, joy accompanied me as I walked."
— Anais Nin

It's never TOO COLD to swim!

"Today, let us swim wildly, joyously in gratitude."
— Rumi

The cold water gets your blood pumping in many unexpected ways and just before you know it, the heat is surging through your veins as you step out of the cold and the air feels soft and caressing.

"You don't make a photograph just with a camera. You bring to the act of photography all the pictures you have seen, the books you have read, the music you have heard, the people you have loved."
— Ansel Adams

A certain stillness creeps in only when we allow for the sun to set, the mists to form and the roots to congregate around our feet.

We then see that there is so much more, hidden between the pathways of silence.

"Sometimes I feel like if you just watch things, just sit still and let the world exist in front of you - sometimes I swear that just for a second time freezes and the world pauses in its tilt. Just for a second. And if you somehow found a way to live in that second, then you would live forever."
— Lauren Oliver

There is a tiny friend who sits on our left shoulder and tells us stories of faraway lands and tales of those who we will never meet. Just when we start to hear that friend is when we start to hear ourselves.

"Life's not about waiting for the storm to pass...
It's about Learning To Dance In The Rain."
— Vivian Greene

"So many things become beautiful when you really look."
— Lauren Oliver

"Nurturing the earthly sounds from fallingwater to crackling fire. These sounds recharge you and bring harmony to your mind, because these are the sounds that have been heard from the start of humankind.
Feel the power of sound that is much older than you, which your ancestors have had as a daily background.
Get back in touch with the sound of nature and silence."
— Karl Tipp

An echo bounches and shimmers above the first-formed ice, thin and fragile like time on a cool river.

The sound of gentle raindrops dance and play one the river like kisses in the soft wind.

"I can elect something I love and absorb myself in it."
— Anais Nin

The process of focusing on crafting a beautiful composition is oftentimes better than the actual thing itself.

"Cinnamon bites and kisses simultaneously."

— Vanna Bonta

"Show me another pleasure like dinner which comes every day and lasts an hour."
— Charles Maurice de Talleyrand

"Remember, sex is like a Chinese dinner. It ain't over 'til you both get your cookie."
— Alec Baldwin

Creativity is more than work. It's allowing your mind become one with the soul. The body will then manifest what you will learn to call art.

WINTER HYGGE

- Hot drinks (masala chai, hot chocolate)
- Good books
- Candle-lit dinners
- Relaxed nights
- Knitwear
- Heartfelt hugs
- Cinnamon bread
- Crisp sugar-coated gingerbread
- Hearthy snowball battle
- Tasty apple pie

Which is your winter hygge?

"The theme of the diary is always the personal, but it does not mean only a personal story: it means a personal relationship to all things and people. The personal, if it is deep enough, becomes universal, mythical, symbolic; I never generalize, intellectualise. I see, I hear, I feel. These are my primitive elements of discovery. Music, dance, poetry and painting are the channels for emotion. It is through them that experience penetrates our bloodstream."
— Anais Nin

"Chirtmas is not a SEASON, it's a FEELING!"
— Edna Ferber

"I want to say words that flame as I say them, but I keep quiet and don't try to make both words fit in one mouthful."
— Rumi

Scent of winter

MASALA CHAI

Masala chai is a creamy, spiced tea beverage made by brewing black tea with a mixture of aromatic Indian spices and herbs.

Chai is typically made with four components:
- Black tea (we prefer bagged or loose-leaf, decaf when possible)
- Spices (ginger, cinnamon, clove, cardamom, black pepper)
- Milk (we went dairy-free with coconut and/or cashew)
- Sweetener (we went for a little maple syrup)

The crushed spices are added to a saucepan with water and freshly grated ginger and left to simmer for about 15 minutes.

It's the perfect drink to enjoy cuddled up with a blanket and a good book.

Warm mittens and hot tea are like twins in an amusement park!

Enjoy!

And don't neglect your To-Do-List ;)

"It's the time you spent on your rose that makes your rose so important... People have forgotten this truth, but you mustn't forget it. You become responsible forever for what you've tamed. You're responsible for your rose."
— Antoine de Saint-Exupéry, The Little Prince

"I like extravagance. Letters which give the postman a stiff back to carry, books which overflow from their covers, sexuality which bursts the thermometers."
— Anais Nin

"Winter, a lingering season, is a time to gather golden moments, embark upon a sentimental journey, and enjoy every idle hour."
— John Boswell

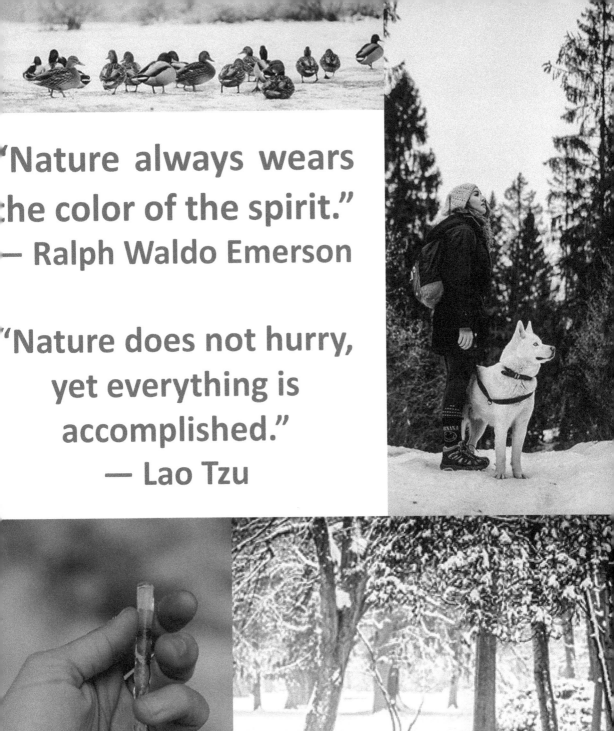

"Nature always wears the color of the spirit."
— Ralph Waldo Emerson

"Nature does not hurry, yet everything is accomplished."
— Lao Tzu

"When words become unclear, I shall focus with photographs. When images become inadequate, I shall be content with silence."

—

Ansel Adams

"to heal
you have to
get to the root
of the wound
and kiss it all the way up"
— Rupi Kaur

"Life is balance of holding on and letting go."
—
Rumi

"Be like a tree and let the dead leaves drop."
—
Rumi

"And don't think the garden loses its ecstasy in winter. It's quiet, but the roots are down there riotous."
— Rumi

Crisp.

Piercing.

Caressing.

Let it flow through You!

"Warm blurr, but preferrably awake. The greater picture somewhere in the background, too murmurred. Awakening deserves celebration.

First drops splash onto toes. A moment of hesitation, if one should. No. Head-on dip with no chance for choice, just the trust in a future wonderous moment.

These moments pass in a limelight, unexpected encounters, which you can only be preperad for during a sigh. Which unchains you. Laughter can ease the greeting of a new day, altough it can be accompanied by a strain, a painful anguish and a sharp punishment. If the present moment weren't a figment of free will, it would be intolerable.

Relaxation would come to mind. Existence would take slimmer measures. Everything passes. Because there are no false moments. Warm embers run across the entire body. But whicheveris infinite?"
— Hanno Padar

SPRING HYGGE

- Planting
- Greeting of spring birds
- The scent of the first spring flowers
- Sunshine and fresh air
- Camping trips outdoors
- Fresh spruce shot tea
- Wild animal gazing
- Easters and egg coloring
- A gust of the first fresh spring breeze
- The lush green scenergy that beholds
- Knowing that life will start to bloom soon!

Which is your spring hygge?

"It's the little details in life that makes all the difference."
— Emilie Barnes

"The bed must be a beautiful place, not only because you make love there but because you dream there as well."
— Anais Nin

Cats have a system for slumber.
You have a system as well...

"I lied and said I was busy.
I was busy;
but not in a way most people understand.

I was busy taking deeper breaths.
I was busy silencing irrational thoughts.
I was busy calming a racing heart.
I was busy telling myself I am OK.

Sometimes this is my busy -
and I will not apologize for it."
— Brittin Oakman

Treat yourself to what you feel.

There is no better time than the present moment!

Homemade Carrot Dumplings

Ingredients
    45 dumpling wrappers
    2 teaspoons potato starch (or cornstarch)

Filling
    1 pound (450 grams) carrots , coarsely chopped
    1 cup dried shiitake mushrooms , rehydrated
    4 cloves garlic
    2 slices ginger
    3 tablespoons sesame oil (or vegetable oil)
    3 large eggs , beaten
    1 cup bamboo shoots , minced
    1/4 teaspoon white pepper powder
    1 tablespoon light soy sauce
    1/2 teaspoon salt

Sauce
    2 tablespoons Chinese black vinegar
    2 teaspoons light soy sauce
    2 teaspoons homemade chili oil (or Sriracha sauce) (Optional)

Prepare The Filling
Rinse shiitake mushrooms and transfer them to a bowl. Add hot water to cover. Rehydrate for 30 minutes, or until tender. Rinse with water again and gently rub by hand to remove dirt from the surface. Drain and set aside.

Add carrots, shiitake mushrooms, garlic, and ginger into a food processor. Pulse until all the ingredients are minced, but not turned to mush.

Heat 2 tablespoons oil in a nonstick skillet over medium heat until warm Add the minced carrot and shiitake mushrooms. Cook and still until the carrot is completely cooked through. Transfer to a large plate to cool.

Heat the remaining 1 tablespoon oil in the same skillet. Add the beaten eggs. Stir and chop the eggs with a spatula, until the eggs are cooked through and turned to small bits. Transfer to a large plate to cool.

When the eggs and carrot mixture have cooled, transfer them to a large bowl. Add bamboo shoot, white pepper powder, light soy sauce, and salt. Mix with a spatula, until everything is mixed well.

It's not a sin if it makes you happy!

Oh, they always know where you've been and where you are going.

Trust is love.

ADD A PERSONAL TOUCH

When creating your room, you definitely want to include some of your own personal touches. This can be any element, smell, sound, or object that particularly soothes your body and relaxes your mind.

Remember, however, that you do not want to overcrowd the space. It is important for a clean and clear environment to keep your mind open. Choose only a few pieces at a time, and swap them out for different ones now and again if you cannot decide.

DIY Candles

Making homemade candles is a fun and easy way to spend an afternoon. These DIY candles make great gifts, or can simply be saved for personal use and enjoyment. This allows for a multitude of possible color combinations. You can even liven things up a bit by adding essential oils to make them scented candles.

- Melt the wax.
- Add fragrance oils.
- Attach the wick.
- Pour the wax
- Cut the wick.

"Treat your relationship as if you are growing the most beautiful sacred flower. Keep watering it, tend to the roots, and always make sure the petals are full of color and are never curling. Once you neglect your plant, it will die, as will your relationship."
— Suzy Kassem

Moments of creation are moments of magic.
Create magic for magic is pure.
So are you!

"Daylight, full of small dancing particles and the one great turning, our souls are dancing with you, without feet, they dance. Can you see them when I whisper in your ear?"
— Rumi

"Dinner is where the magic happens in the kitchen."
— Kris Carr

Did you know that an oven is the magician of hot fresh love?

"One of the very nicest things about life is the way we must regularly stop whatever it is we are doing and devote our attention to eating."
— Luciano Pavarotti

"Always search for your innermost nature in those you are with, as rose oil imbibes from roses."
— Rumi

"Friends can help each other. A true friend is someone who lets you have total freedom to be yourself - and especially to feel. Or, not feel. Whatever you happen to be feeling at the moment is fine with them. That's what real love amounts to - letting a person be what he really is."
— Jim Morrison

Surround yourself with people who love and encourage you. Let them remind you just how amazing you are.

Sing now the lusty song of fruits and flowers.

Herbs come from the earth and guess what happens when we eat them?

"All those spices and herbs in your spice rack can do more than provide calorie-free, natural flavorings to enhance and make food delicious. Theyre also an incredible source of antioxidants and help rev up your metabolism and improve your health at the same time."
— Suzanne Somers

YOU CAN BECOME BLIND
BY SEEING EACH DAY AS A
SIMILAR ONE. EACH DAY IS
A DIFFERENT ONE, EACH
DAY BRINGS A MIRACLE OF
ITS OWN. IT'S JUST A MATTER
OF PAYING ATTENTION TO
THIS MIRACLE.

PAULO COELHO

Matcha

Human kind has known this green tea for over thousands of years. It's known in the "espresso of the tea world" thanks to its taste and envigorating effect.

Farmers grow matcha by covering their tea plants 20–30 days before harvest to avoid direct sunlight. This increases chlorophyll production, boosts the amino acid content, and gives the plant a darker green hue. Once the tea leaves are harvested, the stems and veins are removed and the leaves. Leaves processed this way are called tencha, they are ground into thin powder.

Matcha includes several anti-oxydants like epigallokatechin, which has anti-cancer properties and L-teanin, which helps soothe the mind, restore memory and concentration. The stores often carry two types of matcha tea: usucha (fine grain) and koicha (rough grain), as well as lower propery tea. Usucha is the more common and suits well for daily drinking. Koicha is more often used during official chanoyu tea ceremonies. Samurai Warriors often drank matcha chai to prepare for battle.

Recipe

Use

½ -1tsp of usucha type matcha-powder
120-150 ml 75 degree C water
Add matcha-powder to a warm cha-wan cup or simply a small cup and add water. Whip drink into an even paste. Add the rest of your water and whip vigorously, until tea is nice and

foamy.

Matcha-Latté

Milk turns the matcha tea's flavour int soft and rich.
You can use sweet almond milk or add white chocolate to the drink.
2tsp of matcha-powder and 80C degree water.

Matcha-cake

Add matcha-powder to the dough or on top. 2-3 tsps should make the cake nice and green.

Matcha-milkshake

Ingredients:
1/4 cup of almond milk
2 tsp of culinary matcha
1-2 balls of vanilla ice cream

Gin & Matcha

Gin
Tonic
1g matcha powder
Ice
Rosemary

What can be more refreshing than to drink juice explicitly from mother nature itself?
Tree juice from a birch tree in the very brink of spring can keep you in great health for your whole life!

"I don't have to look up my family tree, because I know that I'm the sap."
— Fred Allen

"Every time you feel lost, confused, think about trees, remember how they grow. Remember that a tree with lots of branches and few roots will get toppled by the first strong wind, while the sap hardly moves in a tree with many roots and few branches. Roots and branches must grow in equal measure, you have to stand both inside of things and above them, because only then will you be able to offer shade and shelter, only then will you be able to cover yourself with leaves and fruit at the proper season. And later on, when so many roads open up before you, you don't know which to take, don't pick one at random; sit down and wait. Breathe deeply, trustingly, the way you breathed on the day when you came into the world, don't let anything distract you, wait and wait some more. Stay still, be quiet, and listen to your heart. Then, when it speaks, get up and go where it takes you."
— Susanna Tamaro

"You have no need to travel anywhere — journey within yourself. Enter a mine of rubies and bathe in the splendor of your own light."

— Rumi

"The time has come to turn your heart into a temple of fire."
— Rumi

„Success isn't a result of spontaneous combustion.
You must set yourself on fire."
— Arnold Glascow

Go for a Walk

Getting out in the fresh air can do you a world of good and promote peace of mind. Take a break and get the blood pumping – especially when the sun is shining.

"I don't like formal gardens. I like wild nature. It's just the wilderness instinct in me, I guess."
- Walt Disney

"I sleep with my feet on moss carpets, my branches in the cotton of the clouds."
- Anais Nin

"And forget not that the earth delights to feel your bare feet and the winds long to play with your hair"
— Khalil Gibran

Come, true life —
embed the experience of life
into your higher clarity.

Life is always where we are.

"Blessed are the curious, for they shall have adventures."
— Lovelle Drachman

Have fun! Get out there and do the things that light your fire. Enjoy them, enjoy being you and enjoy your incredible life.

"The quieter you become, the more you can hear."
— Ram Dass

"A delicate fabric of bird song Floats in the air, The smell of wet wild earth Is everywhere. Oh I must pass nothing by Without loving it much, The raindrop try with my lips, The grass with my touch."
— Sara Teasdale

"Everything in the universe has a rythm, everything dances."

— Maya Angelou

Listen to the birds singing and enjoy the peace and tranquility.

"Let silence take you to the core of life."
— Rumi

"The first creative act is silence."
— Slavoj Žižek

"Dance is the hidden language of the soul."
— Martha Graham

"Dancing is the loftiest, the most moving, the most beautiful of the arts, because it is no mere translation or abstraction from life; it is life itself."
— Havelock Ellis

"The whole world is, to me, very much "alive" - all the little growing things, even the rocks. I can't look at a swell bit of grass and earth, for instancew, without feeling the essential life - the things going on - within them.
The same goes for a mountain, or a bit of the ocean, or a magnificent piece of old wood."
— Ansel Adams

Like two stones connecting.

"Each moment echoes on into infinity"
— Marcus Aurelius

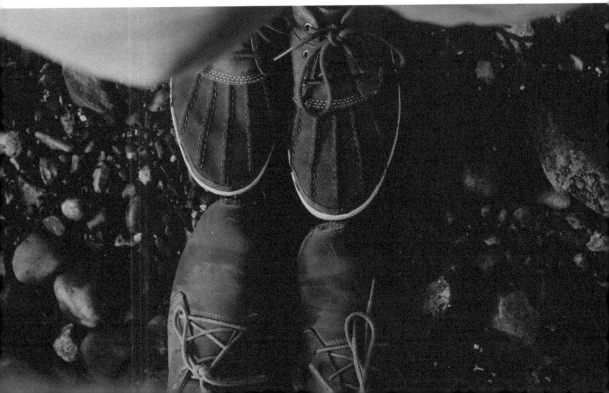

"I prefer to see with closed eyes."
— Josef Albers

"Feelings come and go like clouds in a windy sky.
Conscious breathing is my anchor."
— Thich Nhat Hanh

,,Feelings are much like waves, we can't stop them from coming, but we can choose which one to surf.''
—
Jonatan Mårtensson

"Breathe it all in, love it all out."

— Mary Oliver

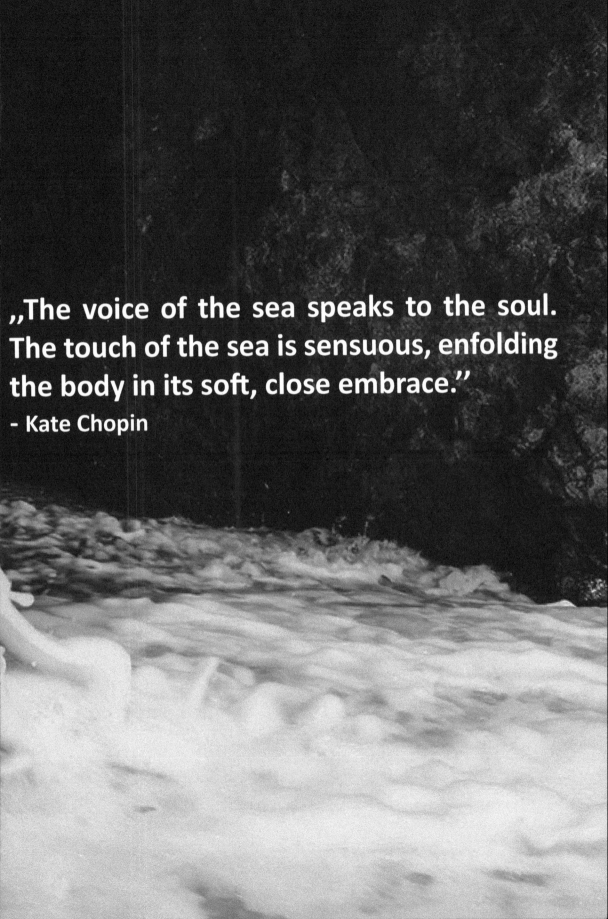

„The voice of the sea speaks to the soul. The touch of the sea is sensuous, enfolding the body in its soft, close embrace."

- Kate Chopin

Love Unconditionally —

Don't do it for love Do it from a place of love.

When you don't expect anything back, it makes it easier to love without fear. When we love with conditions attached, our unmet expectations can create inner turmoil and feelings of resentment. Insecurities destroy peace of mind.

"Our greatest strength lies in the gentleness and tenderness of our heart."
— Rumi

"Realize deeply that the present moment is all you have. Make the NOW the primary focus of your life."
— Eckhart Tolle

Always touch your lover with the attention of the very first time.

Intimacy can fill the soul like a topless chamber in the deepest hallways of the soul. It twirles like a serpent and finds us in the most unexpected epoches of the journeys of our lives.

The sensations are exciting.
Great moments lead to a long night.
Contribution into each other will always bring best returns. Touches and kisses fill the air with a deep musky crave.

Exctasy travels across pulsating veins and pushes strong young blood into both excited bodies. They cannot keep their hands off of each other for hours and hours. Only as the sun rises, they lift their gaze and hot sweaty bodies rest upon each other like the first gentle ocean waves.

"Love one another, but make not a bond of love: let it rather be a moving sea between the shores of your souls.
Fill each other's cup but drink not from one cup. Give one another of your bread but eat not from the same loaf sing and dance together and be joyous, but let each one of you be alone, even as the strings of a lute are alone though they quiver with the same music."
— Kahlil Gibran

"I'm Going to a faraway place, she said... just for a while... her toes wriggled in the warm sand and a silly seagull laughed and danced in the sweet wind."
— My Coconut Island

Throw out your map. The only map you need is you intuition and noone can wrong it. You are a passenger of the great unknown and this is the way life has always been.

The feeling is what counts. Let it linger. Let all your sensations blend into one and then trust that this sensation will carry you on throughout your complete existence.

"Love isn't an emotion or an instinct - it's an art."
— Mae West

"We turn not older with years but newer every day."
— Emily Dickinson

"For sixty years I have been forgetful every minute, but not for a second has this flowing toward me stopped or slowed."
— Rumi

"Life is the dancer and you are the dance."
— Eckhart Tolle

"Dance to inspire, dance to freedom, life is about experiences so dance and let yourself become free."
— Shah Asad Rizvi

"Seek the wisdom that will untie your knot.
Seek the path that demands your whole being."
— Rumi

„Not I, not I, but the wind that blows through me!
A fine wind is blowing the new direction of Time.
If only I let it bear me, carry me, if only it carry
me!"
— D.H. Lawrence

"This poetry. I never know what I'm going to say.
I don't plan it. When I'm outside the saying of it,
I get very quiet and rarely speak at all."
— Rumi

"Let yourself become living poetry."
— Rumi

"Be with those who help your being."
— Rumi

"A warm, rainy day-this is how it feels when friends get together. Friend refreshes friend then, as flowers do each others, in a spring rain."
— Rumi

"The most beautiful things in the world cannot be seen or touched, they are felt with the heart."
— Antoine de Saint-Exupéry, The Little Prince

"Whenever Beauty looks, Love is also there; Whenever beauty shows a rosy cheek Love lights Her fire from that flame. When beauty dwells in the dark folds of night Love comes and finds a heart entangled in tresses. Beauty and Love are as body and soul. Beauty is the mine, Love is the diamond."
— Rumi

"Sing to me in the silence of your heart and I will rise up to hear your triumphant song."
— Rumi

"And silence. She liked the silence most of all. The silence in which the body, senses, the instincts, are more alert, more powerful, more sensitized, live a more richly perfumed and intoxication life."
— Anais Nin

"I love your silences, they are like mine. You are the only being before whom I am not distressed by my own silences. You have a vehement silence, one feels it is charged with essences, it is a strangely alive silence, like a trap open over a well, from which one can hear the secret murmur of the earth itself."
— Anais Nin

A cushion in your soul will take you far. A blanket covering your body can keep you warm. But however strong your spirit is, will determine how high you can fly.

SUMMER HYGGE

- Outdoor concerts, street festivals
- Homemade ice cream
- Picnic in a beautiful place
- Barbeques with friends
- Cold drinks
- Bike rides
- Floral scent
- Making love
- Camping outside
- Midnight bonfires
- Swimming in the warm sea
- Cuddling under the starlit sky

Which is your summer hygge?

A picnic is a state of mind and can be made anywhere.

"Among the delights of Summer were picnics to the woods."
– Georg Brandes

"The best way to remember a beautiful city or a beautiful painting is to eat something while you are looking at it. The flavor really helps the image to penetrate the body."
— Anais Nin

"Smell is a potent wizard that transports you across thousands of miles and all the years you have lived. The odors of fruits waft me to my southern home, to my childhood frolics in the peach orchard. Other odors, instantaneous and fleeting,cause my heart to dilate joyously or contract with remembered grief. Even as I think of smells, my nose is full of scents that start awake sweet memories of summers gone and ripening fields far away."
— Helen Keller

The Spirit Beverage

Its orange is unmistakable, a vibrant color that lights up your toasts and adds extra joy to the moment. Everything else is brought to the table by the inner lighthearted spirit of Aperol Spritz: the same spirit that spontaneously gather people together and sparks nothing but good vibes. This spirit is also contagious: it's difficult to hold back from enjoying a toast with friends, one orange sip at the time.

"Guard well your spare moments. They are like uncut diamonds. Discard them and their value will never be known. Improve them and they will become the brightest gems in a useful life."
— Ralph Waldo Emerson

Be dissolved in your personal power.
Hygge moments accompany your food and your creativity. What you create is what carries you.

What you feed your spiritual body and your physical temple is as important as mindfulness.

Fill your body with food and drink that nourishes it and makes it thrive.

Preparing Fried Kale Crisps

You need:
100g Chunky chopped Kale
1/2 tbsp olive oil
1 heaped tsp of ras el hanout

Heat oven to 150C/130C fan/gas 2 and line 2 baking trays with baking parchment. Wash the kale and dry thoroughly. Drizzle over the oil, then massage into the kale.
Sprinkle over the ras el hanout and some sea salt, mix well, then tip onto the trays and spread out in a single layer. Bake for 18-22 mins or until crisp but still green, then leave to cool for a few mins.

Cooking on live fire keeps the food sizzling.

The natural aromas of a hearthy meal brings out the best in your companions.

"I can trace every romance of my life back to a meal. My memories are enhanced by the tender morsels had at tables across from lovers, on blankets with friends who'd eventually become more, in banquets, barbecues, and breakfasts."
— Stephanie Klein

"Beauty surrounds us, but usually we need to be walking in a garden to know it."
— Rumi

"Everything that slows us down and forces patience, everything that sets us back into the slow circles of nature, is a help. Gardening is an instrument of grace."
— May Sarton

"The ground's generosity takes in our compost and grows beauty! Try to be more like the ground."
— Rumi

Store it with love and it will keep the love for anyone you cherish.

Ingredients

- 3 1/2 quarts water
- 1 cup sugar (regular granulated sugar works best)
- 8 bags black tea, green tea, or a mix (or 2 tablespoons loose tea)
- 2 cups starter tea from last batch of kombucha or store-bought kombucha (unpasteurized, neutral-flavored)
- 1 scoby per fermentation jar, homemade or purchased online

KOMBUCHA

Kombucha is a fermented tea that has been consumed for thousands of years.
Not only does it have the same health benefits as tea — it's also rich in beneficial probiotics.

Ferment for 7 to 10 days: Keep the jar at room temperature, out of direct sunlight, and where it won't get jostled. Ferment for 7 to 10 days, checking the kombucha and the scoby periodically.

A new cream-colored layer of scoby should start forming on the surface of the kombucha within a few days. It usually attaches to the old scoby, but it's ok if they separate. You may also see brown stringy bits floating beneath the scoby, sediment collecting at the bottom, and bubbles collecting around the scoby. This is all normal and signs of healthy fermentation.

After 7 days, begin tasting the kombucha daily by pouring a little out of the jar and into a cup. When it reaches a balance of sweetness and tartness that is pleasant to you, the kombucha is ready to bottle.

Remove the scoby: Before proceeding, prepare and cool another pot of strong tea for your next batch of kombucha, as outlined above. With clean hands, gently lift the scoby out of the kombucha and set it on a clean plate. As you do, check it over and remove the bottom layer if the scoby is getting very thick.

"There is a life-force within your soul, seek that life. There is a gem in the mountain of your body, seek that mine. O traveller, if you are in search of that, don't look outside, look inside yourself and seek that."
— Rumi

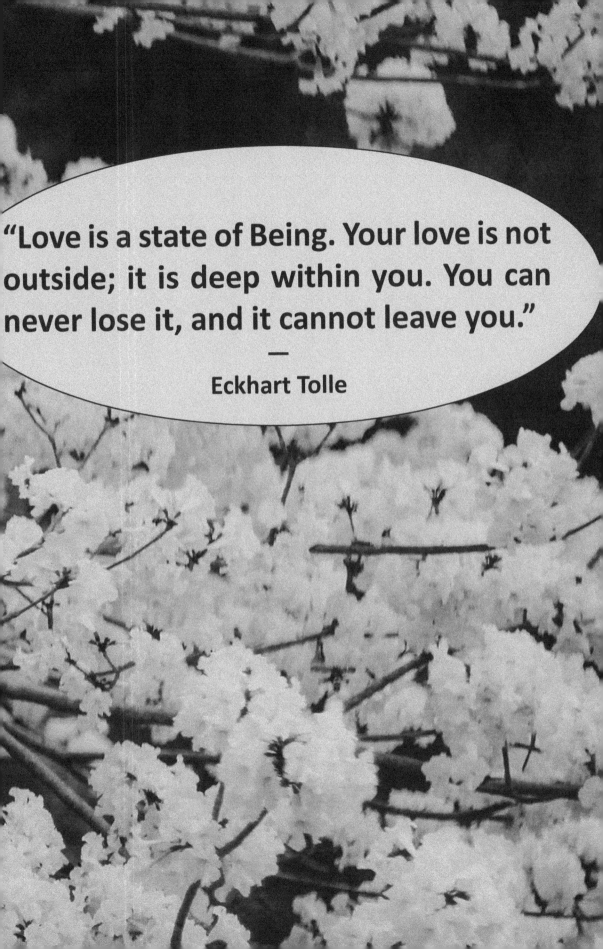

"Love is a state of Being. Your love is not outside; it is deep within you. You can never lose it, and it cannot leave you."
—

Eckhart Tolle

"When I am silent, I fall into the place where everything is music."
—
Rumi

"In summer, the song sings itself."
— W. C. Williams

Lighting is a key element of Hygge. Denmark is a country obsessed with lighting. Lights are used to make spaces feel relaxed and warm.

A candle creates Hygge as it makes the atmosphere more intimate and cozy. The candlelight is not too bright and brings a feeling of comfort. It is a simple kind of daily moment.

HIG...
INSIDE

CARTE DU JOUR

Chocolate uplifts the soul and turns your cheeks rosy. Never forget that.

"Always Share, send good vibes."
— Pranita Deshpande

Who doesn't want to find the bloom with five clovers?

Luck is at your doorstep even if you cannot see it. Just invite it in.

"There are days when the simple act of seeing appears to be true happiness."
— Robert Doisneau

Lavender is the color of intuition. Embrace your true purpose and go with the infinite flow.

Blueberries are a natural way for people to stay healthy.

Love your natural crave for a healthy handful of fruit.

Your blue lips are a part of your eternal transformation!

Flowers bring the scent of homeliness.

Fill your life with the feeling that your home is where your heart feels wonderful.

Your heart holds an epic movie.

Do not fear to share it with
the ones you love the most.

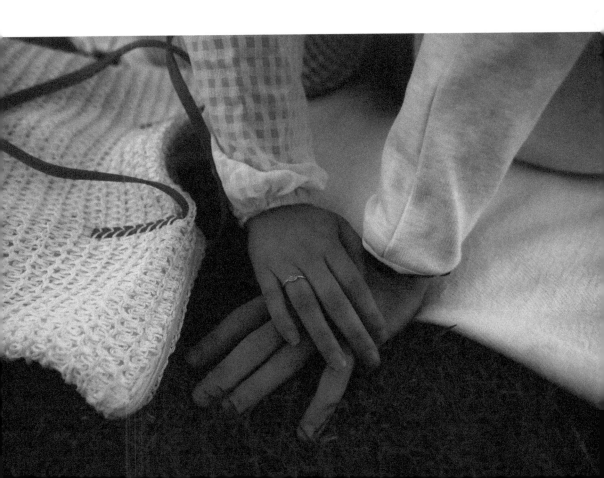

DIY is more than an experience.

It's a shared lifetime.

"Let the beauty we love be what we do."
— Rumi

"You are the artist of your existence, my dear. So color the canvas of your destiny and mold the shape of your reality. Never forget that above all else, your life is a masterpiece of your own creating."
— Becca Lee

,,Dance is that delicacy of life radiating every particle of our existence with happiness."

— Shah Asad Rizvi

XPERIENCE ALL

o be all
hat IS

s the Seed

oday becomes tomorrow
OW is all that is best.

With the present.

„The ocean stirs the heart,
inspires the imagination
and brings eternal joy
to the soul."

—

Wyland

"Only from the heart
can you touch the sky."

—

Rumi

"Water, stories, the body, all the things we do, are mediums that hide and show what's hidden."
— Rumi

"The source is within you. And this whole world is springing up from it."
— Rumi

"What is essential is invisible to the eye"
— Antoine de Saint-Exupéry, The Little Prince

"The work of magic is this, that it breathes and at every breath transforms realities."
— Rumi

"This Love has whispered secrets in your ear that don't make sense to anybody else. You know who You are. You are the shining star."
— Rumi

"So the darkness shall be the light, and the stillness thedancing."
— T.S.Elliot

If wine can make you dance, a shared moment can make you laugh.

"It is possible I never learned the names of birds in order to discover the bird of peace, the bird of paradise, the bird of the soul, the bird of desire. It is possible I avoided learning the names of composers and their music the better to close my eyes and listen to the mystery of all music as an ocean. It may be I have not learned dates in history in order to reach the essence of timelessness. It may be I never learned geography the better to map my own routes and discover my own lands. The unknown was my compass. The unknown was my encyclopedia. The unnamed was my science and progress."
— Anais Nin

"Birdsong brings relief to my longing. I am just as ecstatic as they are, but with nothing to say."
— Rumi

"Dance, and make joyous the love around you.
Dance, and your veils which hide the Light shall swirl
in a heap at your feet."
— Rumi

"Poetry is the alchemy which teaches us to convert ordinary materials into gold."
— Anais Nin

"Poetry, which is our relation to the senses, enables us to retain a living relationship to all things. It is the quickest means of transportation to reach dimensions above or beyond the traps set by the so-called realists. It is a way to learn levitation and travel in liberated continents, to travel by moonlight as well as sunlight."
— Anais Nin

"Painting is silent poetry, and poetry is painting that speaks."
— Plutarch

"All my feelings have the color you desire to paint."
— Rumi

"In your light I learn how to love. In your beauty, how to make poems. You dance inside my chest where no-one sees you, but sometimes I do, and that sight becomes this art."
— Rumi

"The world is full of poetry.
The air is living with its spirit;
and the waves dance to the
music of its melodies, and
sparkle in its brightness."

—

James Gates Percival

"When I paint a still life, I want it to be anything but still, I want it to shimmer with light, I want it to rustle with movement."

—

Henri Matisse

"Good morning," said the little prince.
"Good morning," said the merchant.
This was a merchant who sold pills that had been invented to quench thirst. You need only swallow one pill a week, and you would feel no need for anything to drink.
"Why are you selling those?" asked the little prince.
"Because they save a tremendous amount of time," said the merchant. "Computations have been made by experts. With these pills, you save fifty-three minutes in every week."
"And what do I do with those fifty-three minutes?"
"Anything you like..."
"As for me," said the little prince to himself, "if I had fifty-three minutes to spend as I liked, I should walk at my leisure toward a spring of fresh water."
— Antoine de Saint-Exupéry, The Little Prince

"If the sight of the blue skies fills you with joy, if a blade of grass springing up in the fields has power to move you, if the simple things of nature have a message that you understand, rejoice, for your soul is alive."

— Elonora Duse

"Dancing is not just getting up painlessly, like a leaf blown on the wind; dancing is when you tear your heart out and rise out of your body to hang suspended between the worlds."
— Rumi

"Let your life lightly dance on the edge of time like dew on the tip of a leaf."
— Rabindranath Tagore

MEDICINAL HERBS

- Chamomile
- Lavender
- Ginger
- Peppermint
- Calendula, Pot Marigold
- Echinacea or Purple Coneflower
- Garlic
- Yarrow
- Marigold
- Chamaenerion
- Stinging Nettles
- Spruce thorns

What
makes you
happy?

MORNING HYGGE

Rise Earlier — You gain more time to be with yourself to reflect, meditate or, more importantly, carry out the other morning rituals.

- Stretching in bed, feeling the life energy start to circulate, get the blood pumping
- Bringing yourself in the present moment, noticing everything around. The colors. The smells. The sounds. The touches. The tastes.
- Play with a Pet. Touch is a powerful sense and can ease tension and promote peace of mind.
- Thinking about parts of life and people that make you feel grateful.
- Taking about half an hour to reflect on how you are feeling, creating contact with the self.
- Grab onto your favorite book or just jam to your morning playlist to get tuned to the upcoming day.
- A cold shower brings you perfectly alive, even if it feels a little frightening. Gives a new to breathing.
- Exercising early in the day helps to focus the mind and thoughts and is also usually the one thing that is easy to neglect. In the long term, your body will thank you.

Music effects us on a cellular level.

Even if you're not in a creative mood, music can still appeal to your auditory senses—so have a power playlist or ambient soundscape ready to listen to at home whenever you need a bit of a creative push.

Listen to Uplifting Music

Uplifting music can have a direct impact on our mood, especially in the morning. It charges us emotionally and tunes us into a more positive outlook of the day ahead. It doesn't matter what genre of music you want to listen to, as long as you enjoy it and it makes you feel relaxed.

Gratitude

The real power of gratitude is that it makes you pick out and focus on what is working in your life – what is in tune with your being as a whole. It is selectively positive. It reinforces happiness and positivity by shedding light on those awesome things, small or big, that grace your everyday living.

A little space to be creative

Keeping a personal hygenic routine for a longer period can help create systems in the mind as well.

Maintaining a clear set of things to get your body started is a surefire way to guarantee a great day.

"Let your steps follow you breath, not the other way around."
— Thich Nhat Hanh

"Sometimes the most important thing in a whole day is the rest we take between two deep breaths."
— Etty Hillesum

"Stay kind. It makes you beautiful."

— Najwa Zebian

Self-love is ever evolving. It's something that needs to be practiced daily but can take a lifetime to master. So be kind and support yourself through the hard times.

"As you live Deeper in the Heart, the Mirror gets clearer and cleaner."
— Rumi

Celebrate each and every day and wear the clothes that make your soul blossom!

t's important to fill your spirit with loving, positive and kind images, sounds, smells and tastes.

Great moments uplift us by feeling grateful for the moments in which we feel joy and exctatic fulfilment.

A Serene Paint Palette

Regardless of the color you choose, room color affects your mood, so decide on one that calls to your meditative needs, and makes you feel calm and relaxed.

EVENING RITUALS

The purpose of bedtime routines is to relax and de-stress.
- A long walk. It helps your mind cool down.
- Music is food for the soul and an instant way to gain peace of mind.
- Take a hot shower or soak in the bath.
- Body-peeling procedures and applying creme.
- Enjoy a refreshing deep frozen orange slice.
- Meditation gives space and perspective to calm those racing thoughts that rob you of a good night's sleep.
- Keeping a diary helps you unwind and write off the day to help empty the mind.
- Surrounding oneself is an ancient ritual for grounding the spirit.
- Feel the gratitude for all that is in your life.
- Clean bed clothes.
- Fresh air.
- Relaxing Incenses.
- A Soothing tea.
- Stretch.
- An exhilarating read.
- Deep Breathing.

Embrace the moment.

Release the foam bubbles into the air without a flicker of worry whether the bubbles break or travel far beyond their reach.

Take time out to calm your mind every day. Breathe in and out, clear your mind of your thoughts and just be.

"Masturbation is a meditation on self-love. So many of us are afflicted with self-loathing, bad body images, shame about our body functions, and confusion about sex and pleasure, I recommend an intense love affair with yourself."
— Betty Dodson

Feel free to express your
secret wants and wishes.

'The body is an instrument which only gives off music when it is used as a body. Always an orchestra, and just as music traverses walls, so sensuality traverses the body and reaches up to ecstasy."
— Anais Nin

'Passion gives me moments of wholeness."
— Anais Nin

"What everyone forgets is that passion is not merely a heightened sensual fusion but a way of life which produces, as in the mystics, an ecstatic awareness of the whole of life."
— Anais Nin

"Expressing feelings is linked directly with creation... In this ability to tap the sources of feeling and imagination lies the secret of abundance."
— Anais Nin

"I don't hear your words: your voice reverberates against my body like another kind of caress, another kind of penetration. I have no power over your voice. It comes straight from you into me. I could stuff my ears and it would find its way into my blood and make it rise."
— Anais Nin

The more we like ourselves, the greater our peace of mind. We accept ourselves more and feel at ease in the world, no matter what situation we find ourselves in. We experience less insecurity and as a result, our inner peace is heightened.

Get in touch with your inner dialogue. If it's anything less than loving, encouraging and supportive, it's time to make a change. You deserve to be spoken to in the same way you would speak to your best friend, sister, brother, daughter, or son.

"Self-care is never a selfish act – it is simply good steward ship of the only gift I have, the gift I was put on earth to offer others. Anytime we can listen to true self and give the care it requires, we do it not only for ourselves, but for the many others whose lives we touch."
— Parker Palmer

Self
Love

"This is my home, you see, so no longer will I let it be a place of shame or a vessel of insecurity. It will be my chapel of forgiveness and a palace of respect."
— Becca Lee

Pamper Yourself

Move that gorgeous body of yours every single day and learn to love the skin you're in. You can't hate your way into loving yourself.
Self-care is anything that enhances your mood increases your vitality supports your well-being.
Make a commitment to loving yourself on a deeper level. Pampering yourself may be one of the most pleasurable self-care acts to make a priority in your life.

Do you know that the words meditation and medicine come from the same root? Meditation is a kind of medicine; its use is only for the time being.
Once you have learned the quality, then you need not do any particular meditation, then the meditation has to spread all over your life.
Only when you are meditative twenty-four hours a day then can you attain, then you have attained.
Even sleeping is meditation.

"These are the qualities of meditation: a really meditative person is playful; life is fun for him, life is a leela, a play. He enjoys it tremendously. He is not serious. He is relaxed."

—

OSHO

Find a quiet and peaceful place.
Put on clean and comfortable clothing.
Turn off all the gadgets and electronic items;
Choose the music for your meditation.
Light candles, rose essential oil or incense.
Sit in a comfortable position
and take a few deep breaths

MEDITATION

Meditation is just to be, not doing anything – no action, no thought, no emotion. You just are. And it is a sheer delight. From where does this delight come when you are not doing anything? It comes from nowhere, or, it comes from everywhere. It is uncaused, because the existence is made of the stuff called joy. It needs no cause, no reason. If you are unhappy you have a reason to be unhappy; if you are happy you are simply happy – there is no reason for it. Your mind tries to find a reason because it cannot believe in the uncaused, because it cannot control the uncaused – with the uncaused the mind simply becomes impotent. So the mind goes on finding some reason or other. But I would like to tell you that whenever you are happy, you are happy for no reason at all, whenever you are unhappy, you have some reason to be unhappy – because happiness is just the stuff you are made of. It is your very being, it is your innermost core. Joy is your innermost core."
– OSHO

Sage and Palo Santo are typically used to cleanse a space of negative energy, while incense brings in a specific scent blend to shift energy and elevate your mood (think aromatherapy).

Aromatherapy

The use of essential oils from plants, such as lavender, chamomile, and peppermint, can really soothe the soul, the mind, and the body.

From burning candles and incense, to heating oils, you can receive the benefits of aromatherapy while medicating. Aside from the aromatherapy smells you have in the room, you also want to make sure you have fresh air.

Homemade essential oil air fresheners

The number of home fragrance products available today is staggering. There are scented candles, potpourri, scented sprays, oil diffusers, incense and plug-in room deodorizers. But before shelling out for products that contain a host of potentially harmful toxins and chemicals, consider making your own air fresheners. A few drops of highly concentrated essential oils can add a lovely dose of natural fragrance to your home.

Homemade oil diffusers

Oil diffusers are a great way to infuse your home with a continuous and subtle scent.
- *A small, clean jar. A container with a wide base and a small opening works best, as they discourage evaporation.*
- *Reeds.*
- *Mineral oil. Mineral oil is less viscous than vegetable oil and is better at carrying the scent up the reeds.*
- *Vodka. Plain, unflavored, nondiluted vodka. The vodka helps thin out the oil so that it will move more easily up the reeds.*
- *Essential oil(s).*

How to assemble your oil diffuser:
- *Pour one-quarter cup mineral oil and two tablespoons vodka into a measuring cup and stir well to combine the liquids.*
- *Add in one and one-half tablespoons of essential oil (the ratio should be about one part essential oil to four parts mineral oil and vodka).*
- *Stir well and pour the oil mixture into your container. Insert as many reeds as will fit into the opening.*
- *Flip the reeds every few days to optimize the scent diffusion.*

Homemade air freshening spray

When your home needs a instant refresh, nothing is quicker and easier than a spritz of air freshener.
You will need:
- *A clean, empty spray bottle*
- *Water*
- *Vodka (unflavored and nondiluted)*
- *Essential oil*

How to make your air freshening spray:
- *Pour one cup of water into a clean, reusable spray bottle.*
- *Add in two tablespoons of vodka and about 20 drops of essential oils (keep in mind that some essential oils are stronger than others, so start off conservatively when adding the oil).*
- *Screw on the top and shake well to combine the mixture.*

If you haven't used essential oils before, don't be afraid to jump in.

Nature is organically relaxing and healing, so it only makes sense that you bring some natural elements into the room where you want to relax and meditate.

You can choose any natural elements you prefer. This could be a plant, a vase of cut flowers, or even a small water fountain. If you can't meditate on the beach while the sounds of the changing ocean tides fill your ears, at least a small, indoor waterfall will offer similar soothing sounds (and will drown out the sounds of the bustling city outside your doors).

Aloe vera may be a source of natural treatment for a variety of skin ailments.

You can easily grow your own plants and they will bring you joy in so many ways: cuts, frost bite, burns, dry skin, akne, psoriasis, eczema and so on.

Oatmeal & Honey Soap

n this homemade soap, oatmeal — known for its
naturally exfoliating and skin-soothing properties—
s the star ingredient.
A shea butter soap base and raw honey make these
bar soaps even more nourishing for the skin.

- You must have an accurate digital scale to make soap.
- 16 ounces coconut oil
- 40 ounces olive oil
- 16-21 ounces distilled water
- 7.86 ounces lye (sodium hydroxide)
- At trace add: 1 tablespoons ground oats, 1/2 tablespoon
  honey, plus an extra tablespoon oil or butter.
- Optional: add 15 drops lavender essential oil

Gua sha is a natural, alternative therapy that involves scraping your skin with a massage tool to improve your circulation. This ancient Chinese healing technique may offer a unique approach to better health, addressing issues like chronic pain.

Gua sha is intended to address stagnant energy, called chi, in the body that practitioners believe may be responsible for inflammation. Inflammation is the underlying cause of several conditions associated with chronic pain. Rubbing the skin's surface is thought to help break up this energy, reduce inflammation, and promote healing.

Facial Gua Sha is a massage technique designed to relieve tension in the muscles of the face, boost blood circulation, and encourage lymphatic drainage to banish bloat. It helps break up fascia, the connective tissue that hugs muscles but can sometimes interfere with optimal circulation.

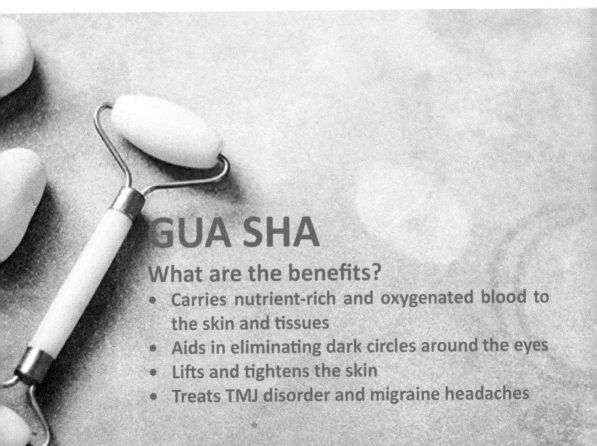

GUA SHA

What are the benefits?

- Carries nutrient-rich and oxygenated blood to the skin and tissues
- Aids in eliminating dark circles around the eyes
- Lifts and tightens the skin
- Treats TMJ disorder and migraine headaches

MACRAMÉ

Macramé is a form of textile produced using knotting (rather than weaving or knitting) techniques.

Materials used in macramé include cords made of cotton wine, linen, hemp, jute, leather or yarn. Cords are iden-ified by construction, such as a 3-ply cord, made of three engths of fibre twisted together.

Cavandoli macramé is one variety that is used to form geometric and free-form patterns like weaving. The Ca-vandoli style is done mainly in a single knot, the double half-hitch knot. Reverse half hitches are sometimes used to maintain balance when working left and right halves of a balanced piece.

To behave playfully and uninhibitedly.

Approach life with a playful attitude. When did you last let the child in you come out to play?

Children
are
the
petals
of the flower
of our lives.

The precious moments spent with our lovely children are the dearest gems of memories.

Every one of these moments is unique and will linger on with you. Just know that you are a good mother. You're giving your best.

Let us be grateful to people who make us happy, they are the charming gardeners who make our soul blossom.
— Marcel Proust

Making you own citrus cleaning solution!

Ingredients:
3-5 citrus fruits (lemons/oranges/grapefruits)
0,5 l distilled vinegar

Peel the citrus fruits and add the peels to a sealable jar. Add the distilled vinegar so that the vinegar does not seap out. Keep the peals and vinegar in a har for 4 weeks. Now, your cleaning solution is ready. Pour it out into a spray bottle and clean all your precious surfaces!

lave regular clear-outs. Clutter can add to feelings of tension nd a clean, clear home allows a clearer, more peaceful mind.

learing out and organizing your space at home helps make oom for new things—and new ideas.

ood way to get your creative thoughts flowing is to engage in a imple, but stimulating, activity such as washing the dishes.

FENG SHUI

Broken Dishes

At the first sign of a chip, you should toss your teacup, plate, or bowl. Why? Well, according to Feng Shui practices, dishes symbolize wealth and family. When you eat on cracked plates, you'll subconsciously welcome troubles and failures into your life.

KINTSUGI

Kintsugi ("golden joinery"), also known as Kintsukuroi ("golden repair"), is the Japanese art of repairing broken pottery by mending the areas of breakage with lacquer dusted or mixed with powdered gold, silver, or platinum, a method similar to the maki-e technique. As a philosophy, it treats breakage and repair as part of the history of an object, rather than something to disguise.

Kintsugi can relate to the Japanese philosophy of "no mind", which encompasses the concepts of non-attachment, acceptance of change, and fate as aspects of human life.

" Not only is there no attempt to hide the damage, but the repair is literally illuminated... a kind of physical expression of the spirit of mushin... Mushin is often literally translated as "no mind," but carries connotations of fully existing within the moment, of non-attachment, of equanimity amid changing conditions. ...The vicissitudes of existence over time, to which all humans are susceptible, could not be clearer than in the breaks, the knocks, and the shattering to which ceramic ware too is subject. This poignancy or aesthetic of existence has been known in Japan as mono no aware, a compassionate sensitivity, or perhaps identification with, outside oneself."
—Christy Bartlett, Flickwerk: The Aesthetics of Mended Japanese Ceramics

Tea ceremony is a way of worshipping the beautiful and the simple. All one's efforts are concentrated on trying to achieve perfection through the imperfect gestures of daily life. Its beauty consists in the respect with which it is performed. If a mere cup of tea can bring us closer to God, we should watch out for all the other dozens of opportunities that each ordinary day offers us."
— Paulo Coelho

ound Therapy uses sound, music and specialist instruments played in therapeutic ways, combined with deep self-reflection techniques to improve health and wellbeing.

The therapeutic sound and sound therapy techniques are delivered using tonal and rhythmic instruments and voice. The tonal instruments used are Himalayan and crystal singing bowls, gongs and tuning forks. The vocal techniques are toning (the singing of one tone – usually using a vowel sound), overtoning (a technique where more than one tone is sung simultaneously) or mantra (the chanting of Sanskrit words). A practitioner of Holistic Voice Therapy or Group Voice Therapy may also use 'Vocal Processing Techniques' which combine movement, breath and visualisation as well as voice. A therapeutic rhythm treatment/session is given using frame drum and therapeutic percussion comprises rainsticks, shakers, chimes and other percussion tools delivered in a specific order to maximise the therapeutic process.

"Because I cannot sleep
I make music in the night."
—

Rumi

GREAT NIGHTTIME

A Particular
TIME OF The AWAKENED

It's The Time of SILENCE
—

WHIM OF CREATION

Good Night!